David Mamet

GLENGARRY GLEN ROSS

A play in two acts

METHUEN · LONDON

First published 1984 in simultaneous hardback and paperback
editions by Methuen London Ltd.,
11 New Fetter Lane, London EC4P 4EE
Copyright © 1984 by David Mamet
Set in IBM 10 point Journal by 🅰 Tek-Art, Croydon, Surrey

Printed in Great Britain by
Richard Clay (The Chaucer Press) Ltd,
Bungay, Suffolk

British Library Cataloguing in Publication Data
Mamet, David
    Glengarry Glen Ross. — (Methuen modern plays)
    I. Title
    812'.54   PS3563.A435

ISBN 0-413-55410-4
ISBN 0-413-55420-1 Pbk

CAUTION
All rights in this play are strictly reserved and application for
performance etc., should be made before rehearsal to
Rosenstone/Wender, 3 East 48th Street, New York City 10017,
USA. No performance may be given unless a licence has been
obtained.

This play is dedicated to Harold Pinter.

Glengarry Glen Ross was first presented in the Cottesloe auditorium of the National Theatre, London, on 21 September, 1983, with the following cast:

SHELLY LEVENE, *fifties*	Derek Newark
JOHN WILLIAMSON, *forties*	Karl Johnson
DAVE MOSS, *fifties*	Trevor Ray
GEORGE AARONOW, *fifties*	James Grant
RICHARD ROMA, *forties*	Jack Shepherd
JAMES LINGK, *forties*	Tony Haygarth
BAYLEN, *forties*	John Tams

Directed by Bill Bryden
Designed by Hayden Griffin
Lighting by Andy Phillips
Sound by Caz Appleton

The three scenes of Act One take place in a Chinese restaurant. Act Two takes place in a real estate office.

Author's Note

David Mamet himself worked for a while in a real estate office in 1969. Here are his comments describing that time.

The office was a fly-by-night operation which sold tracts of undeveloped land in Arizona and Florida to gullible Chicagoens. The firms advertised on radio and television and their pitch was to this effect: 'Get in on the ground floor . . . Beautiful home-sites in scenic/historic Arizona/Florida. For more information call . . . for our beautiful brochure.' Interested viewers would telephone in for the brochure and their names and numbers were given to me. My job was to call them back, assess their income and sales susceptibility, and arrange an appointment with them for one of the office salesmen.

This appointment was called a *lead* — in the same way that a clue in a criminal case is called a *lead* — ie. it may lead to the suspect, the suspect in this case being a *prospect*. It was then my job to gauge the relative worth of these leads and assign them to the salesforce. The salesmen would then take their assigned leads and go out on the appointments, which were called *sits* . . . ie. a meeting where one actually *sits down* with the prospects . . .

So that's the background to the play. We are in a real estate office. There is a sales contest near its end. The four salesmen have only several more days to establish their position on the sales graph, the *board*. The top man wins a Cadillac, the second man wins a set of steak knives, the bottom two men get fired. The competition centres around the *leads*, with each man trying desperately to get the best ones.

Always be closing

Practical sales maxim

Act One

ACT ONE

Scene One

A booth at a Chinese restaurant, WILLIAMSON *and* LEVENE *are seated at the booth.*

LEVENE. John . . . John . . . John. Okay. John. John. Look: (*Pause.*) The Glengarry Highland's leads, you're sending Roma out. Fine. He's a good man. We know that he is. He's fine. All I'm saying, you look at the *board,* he's throwing . . . <u>wait, wait, wait</u>, he's throwing them *away,* he's throwing the leads away. All that I'm saying, that you're wasting leads. I don't want to tell you your *job.* All that I'm saying, things get *set,* I know they do, you get a certain *mindset* . . . A guy gets a reputation. We know how this . . . all I'm saying, put a *closer* on the job. There's more than one man for the . . . Put a . . . wait a second, put a *proven man out* . . . and you watch, now *wait* a second — and you watch your *dollar* volumes . . . You start closing them for *fifty* 'stead of *twenty-five* . . . you put a *closer* on the . . .

WILLIAMSON. Shelly, you blew the last . . .

LEVENE. No. John. No. Let's wait, let's back up here, I did . . . will you please? Wait a second. Please. I didn't 'blow' them. No. I didn't 'blow' them. No. One kicked *out,* one I *closed* . . .

WILLIAMSON. . . . you didn't close . . .

LEVENE. . . . I, if you'd *listen* to me. Please. I *closed* the cocksucker. His *'ex'*, John, his *ex, I* didn't know he was married . . . he, the *judge* invalidated the . . .

WILLIAMSON. Shelly . . .

3

LEVENE. . . . and what is that, John? What? Bad *luck*. That's all it is. I pray in your *life* you will never find it runs in streaks. That's what it does, that's all it's doing. Streaks. I pray it misses you. That's all I want to say.

WILLIAMSON (*pause*). What about the other two?

LEVENE. What two?

WILLIAMSON. Four. You had four leads. One kicked out, one the *judge*, you say . . .

LEVENE. . . . you want to see the court records? John? Eh? You want to go down. . .

WILLIAMSON. . . . no . . .

LEVENE. . . . do you want to go down-*town* . . .?

WILLIAMSON. . . . no . . .

LEVENE. . . . then . . .

WILLIAMSON. . . . I only . . .

LEVENE. . . . then what is this 'you *say*' shit, what is that? (*Pause*.) What is that . . .?

WILLIAMSON. All that I'm saying . . .

LEVENE. What is this 'you *say*'? A deal kicks out . . . I got to *eat. Shit*, Williamson . . . *Shit You*, Moss . . . Roma . . . look at the *sheets* . . . look at the *sheets*. Nineteen *eighty*, eighty-*one* . . . eighty-*two* . . . six months of eighty-two . . . who's there? Who's up there?

WILLIAMSON. Roma.

LEVENE. Under him?

WILLIAMSON. Moss.

LEVENE. Bullshit. John. Bull*shit*. April, September 1981. It's *me*. It isn't *fucking* Moss. Due respect, he's an *order* taker, John. He *talks*, he talks a good game, look at the *board*, and it's *me*, John, it's me . . .

WILLIAMSON. Not lately it isn't.

LEVENE. Lately kiss my ass lately. That isn't how you build an org . . . talk, talk to Murray. Talk to Mitch. When we were on Peterson, who paid for his fucking *car*? You talk to him. The *Seville* . . .? He came in, 'You bought that for me Shelly.' Out of *what*? Cold *calling. Nothing.* Sixty-*five,* when we were there, with Glen Ross *Farms*? You call 'em down-town. What was that? *Luck*? That was 'luck'? *Bullshit,* John. You're luck — burning my ass, I can't get a fucking *lead* . . . you think that was luck. My stats for those years? Bull*shit* . . . over that period of time . . .? Bull*shit*. It wasn't luck. It was *skill.* You want to throw that away, John . . .? You want to throw that away?

WILLIAMSON. It isn't me . . .

LEVENE. . . . it isn't you . . .? Who *is* it? Who is this I'm talking to? I need the *leads* . . .

WILLIAMSON. . . . after the thirtieth . . .

LEVENE. Bull*shit* the thirtieth, I don't get on the board the thirtieth, they're going to can my ass. I need the leads. I need them now. Or I'm gone, and you're going to miss me, John, I swear to you.

WILLIAMSON. Murray . . .

LEVENE. . . . you *talk* to Murray . . .

WILLIAMSON. I have. And my job is to marshall those leads . . .

LEVENE. Marshall the leads . . . marshall the leads? What the fuck, what bus did *you* get off of, we're here to fucking *sell. Fuck* marshalling the leads. What the fuck talk is that? What the fuck talk is that? Where did you learn that? In school . . .? (*Pause.*) That's 'talk', my friend, that's 'talk'. Our job is to *sell.* I'm the *man* to sell. I'm getting garbage. (*Pause.*) You're giving it to me, and what I'm saying is it's *fucked.*

WILLIAMSON. You're saying that I'm fucked.

LEVENE. Yes. (*Pause.*) I am. I'm sorry to antagonize you.

WILLIAMSON. Let me . . .

LEVENE. . . . and I'm going to get bounced and you're . . .

WILLIAMSON. . . . let me . . . are you listening to me . . .?

LEVENE. Yes.

WILLIAMSON. Let me tell you something, Shelly. I do what I'm hired to do. I'm . . . wait a second. I'm *hired* to watch the leads. I'm given . . . hold on, I'm given a *policy. My* job is to *do that.* What I'm *told.* That's it. You, wait a second, *anybody* falls below a certain mark I'm not *permitted* to give them the premium leads.

LEVENE. Then how do they come up above that mark? With *dreck* . . .? That's *nonsense.* Explain this to me. Cause it's a waste, and it's a stupid waste. I want to tell you something . . .

WILLIAMSON. You know what those leads cost?

LEVENE. The premium leads. Yes. I know what they cost. John. Because I, *I* generated the dollar revenue sufficient to *buy* them. Nineteen senny-*nine,* you know what I made? Senny-*Nine?* Ninety-six thousand dollars. John? For *Murray* . . . For *Mitch* . . . look at the sheets . . .

WILLIAMSON. Murray said . . .

LEVENE. *Fuck* him. *Fuck* Murray. John? You know? You tell him I said so. What does *he* fucking know? He's going to have a 'sales' contest . . . you know what our sales contest used to be? *Money.* A *fortune.* Money lying on the ground. Murray? When was the last time *he* went out on a sit? Sales contest? It's *laughable.* It's cold out there now, John. It's tight. Money is *tight.* This ain't sixty-five. It ain't. It just ain't. See? See? Now, I'm a good *man* — but I need a . . .

WILLIAMSON. Murray said . . .

LEVENE. John. John . . .

WILLIAMSON. Will you please wait a second. Shelly. Please. Murray told me: The hot leads . . .

LEVENE. . . . ah, *fuck* this . . .

WILLIAMSON. The . . . Shelly . . .? (*Pause.*) The hot leads are assigned according to the board. During the contest. *Period.* Anyone who beats fifty per . . .

LEVENE. That's fucked. That's fucked. You don't look at the fucking *percentage*. You look at the *gross* . . .

WILLIAMSON. Either way. You're out.

LEVENE. I'm out.

WILLIAMSON. Yes.

LEVENE. I'll tell you why I'm out. I'm *out,* you're giving me toilet paper. John. I've *seen* those leads. I saw them when I was at Homestead, we pitched those cocksuckers Rio Rancho nineteen sixty-*nine* they wouldn't buy. They couldn't buy a fucking *toaster.* They're *broke,* John. They're cold. They're deadbeats, you can't judge on that. Even so. Even so. Alright. Fine. Fine. Even so. I go in, FOUR FUCKING LEADS they got their money in a *sock.* They're fucking *Polacks,* John. Four leads. I close two. *Two.* Fifty per . . .

WILLIAMSON. . . . they kicked out . . .

LEVENE. They *all* kick out. You run in *streaks,* pal. *Streaks.* I'm . . . I'm . . . don't look at the *board,* look at *me.* Shelly Levene. *Anyone. Ask* them on Western. Ask Getz at Homestead. Go ask Jerry Graff. You know who I am . . . I NEED A SHOT. I got to get on the fucking board. Ask them. *Ask* them. Ask them who ever picked up a check I was flush. Moss, Jerry Graff, Mitch himself . . . Those guys *lived* on the business I brought in. They *lived* on it . . . and so did Murray, John. You were here you'd of benefitted from it too. And now I'm saying this. Do I want charity? Do I want *pity?* I want *sits.* I want leads don't come right out of a *phonebook.* Give me a lead hotter than that, I'll go in and close it. Give me a chance. That's all I want. I'm going to *get* up on that fucking board and all I want is a chance. It's a *streak* and I'm going to turn it around. (*Pause.*) I need your help. (*Pause.*)

WILLIAMSON. I can't do it, Shelly.

Pause.

LEVENE. Why?

WILLIAMSON. The leads are assigned randomly . . .

LEVENE. *Bullshit, Bullshit,* you assign them . . . What are you *telling* me?

WILLIAMSON. . . . apart from the top men on the contest board.

LEVENE. Then put me on the board.

WILLIAMSON. You start closing again, you'll *be* on the board.

LEVENE. I can't close these leads, John. No one can. It's a joke. Look, look: you put me in with Roma — we'll go out together, him and me, we'll doubleteam 'em . . .

WILLIAMSON. Dream on.

LEVENE. Okay. Okay . . . Just . . . (*Pause.*) John, look: just give me a hot lead. Just give me two of the premium leads. As a 'test', alright? As a 'test'. And I promise you . . .

WILLIAMSON. I can't do it, Shel . . .

LEVENE. I'll give you ten per cent.

Pause.

WILLIAMSON. Of what?

LEVENE. Of my end what I close.

WILLIAMSON. And what if you don't close?

LEVENE. I *will* close.

WILLIAMSON. What if you *don't* close . . .?

LEVENE. I *will* close.

WILLIAMSON. What if you *don't*? Then I'm *fucked*. You see . . .? Then it's *my* job. That's what I'm *telling* you.

LEVENE. I *will* close. John, John, ten per cent. I can get hot. You *know* that . . .

WILLIAMSON. Not lately you can't . . .

LEVENE. Fuck that. That's defeatist. Fuck that. Fuck it . . . Get on my side. *Go* with me. Let's *do* something. You want to run this office, *run* it.

WILLIAMSON. Twenty per cent.

Pause.

LEVENE. Alright.

WILLIAMSON. And fifty bucks a lead.

LEVENE. John . . . (*Pause.*) Listen. I want to talk to you.

Permit me to do this a second. I'm older than you. A man acquires a reputation. On the street. What he does when he's *up,* what he does otherwise . . . I said 'ten', you said 'no'. You said 'twenty'. I said 'fine', I'm not going to fuck with you, how can I beat that, you tell me? . . . Okay. Okay. We'll . . . Okay. Fine. We'll . . . Alright, twenty per cent, and fifty bucks a lead. That's fine. For now. That's fine. A month or two we'll talk. A month from now. Next month. After the thirtieth. (*Pause.*) We'll talk.

WILLIAMSON. What are we going to say?

LEVENE. No. You're right. That's for later. We'll talk in a month. What have you got? I want two sits. Tonight.

WILLIAMSON. I'm not sure I have two.

LEVENE. I saw the board. You've got *four* . . .

WILLIAMSON (*snaps*). I've got *Roma.* Then I've got Moss . . .

LEVENE. *Bullshit.* They ain't been in the office yet. Give 'em some stiff. We have a deal or not? Eh? Two sits. The Des Plaines. Both of 'em, six and ten, you can do it . . . six and ten . . . eight and eleven, I don't give a shit, you set 'em up? Alright? The two sits in Des Plaines.

WILLIAMSON. Alright.

LEVENE. Good. Now we're talking.

Pause.

WILLIAMSON. A hundred bucks.

Pause.

LEVENE. Now? (*Pause.*) *Now?*

WILLIAMSON. Now. (*Pause.*) Yes . . . *When?*

LEVENE. Ah, *shit,* John . . .

Pause.

WILLIAMSON. I wish I could.

LEVENE. You fucking asshole . . . (*Pause.*) I haven't got it. (*Pause.*) I haven't got it, John. (*Pause.*) I'll pay you tomorrow. (*Pause.*) I'm coming in here with the sales, I'll

pay you *tomorrow*. (*Pause*.) I haven't *got* it, when I pay,
the *gas* . . . I get back to the hotel, I'll bring it in tomorrow.

WILLIAMSON. Can't do it.

LEVENE. I'll give you thirty on them now, I'll bring the rest
tomorrow. I've got it at the hotel. (*Pause*.) John? (*Pause*.)
We do that, for chrissake?

WILLIAMSON. No.

LEVENE. I'm asking you. As a favor to me? (*Pause*.) John.
(*Long pause*.) John: my *daughter* . . .

WILLIAMSON. I can't do it, Shelly.

LEVENE. Well, I want to tell you something, fella, wasn't
long I could pick up the phone, call *Murray* and I'd have
your job. You know that? Not too *long* ago. For what? For
nothing. 'Mur, this new kid burns my ass.' 'Shelly, he's out.'
You're gone before I'm back from lunch. I bought him a trip
to Bermuda once . . .

WILLIAMSON. I have to go . . . (*He gets up*.)

LEVENE. Wait. Alright. Fine. (*He starts going in his pocket for
money*.) The one. Give me the lead. Give me the one lead.
The best one you have.

WILLIAMSON. I can't split them.

Pause.

LEVENE. Why?

WILLIAMSON. Because I say so.

LEVENE. (*pause*). Is that it? Is that *it*? You want to do business
that way . . .?

WILLIAMSON *gets up, leaves money on the table*.

You want to do business that way . . .? Alright. Alright.
Alright. Alright. What is there on the other list . . .?

WILLIAMSON. You want something off the B list?

LEVENE. *Yeah*. Yeah.

WILLIAMSON. Is that what you're saying?

LEVENE. That's what I'm saying. Yeah. (*Pause*.) I'd like

something off the other list. Which, very least, that I'm
entitled to. If I'm still *working* here which for the moment I
guess that I am . . . (*Pause.*) What? I'm sorry I spoke harshly
to you.

WILLIAMSON. That's alright.

LEVENE. The deal still stands, our other thing.

WILLIAMSON *shrugs; starts out of the booth.*

Good. Mmm. I, you know, I left my wallet back at the
hotel. Alright. Mmm. (*Pause.*) Mmm . . . Fine.

Scene Two

A booth at the restaurant. MOSS *and* AARONOW *seated. After
the meal.*

MOSS. Polacks and deadbeats.

AARONOW. . . . Polacks . . .

MOSS. Deadbeats *all.*

AARONOW. . . . they hold on to their money . . .

MOSS. All of 'em. They, *hey:* it happens to us all.

AARONOW. Where am I going to work?

MOSS. You have to cheer up, George, you aren't out yet.

AARONOW. I'm not?

MOSS. You missed a fucking sale. Big deal. A deadbeat Polack.
Big deal. How you going to sell 'em in the *first* place . . .?
Your mistake, you shoun'a took the lead.

AARONOW. I had to.

MOSS. You had to, yeah. Why?

AARONOW. To get on the . . .

MOSS. To get on the board. Yeah. How you goan a get on the
board sell'n a Polack? And I'll tell you, I'll tell you what *else*.
You listening? I'll tell you what else: don't ever try to sell an
Indian.

AARONOW. I'd never try to sell an Indian.

MOSS. You get those names come up, you ever get 'em, 'Patel'?

AARONOW. *Mmm* . . .

MOSS. You ever get 'em?

AARONOW. Well, I think I had one once.

MOSS. You did?

AARONOW. I . . . I don't know.

MOSS. You had one you'd know it. *Patel.* They keep coming up. I don't know. They like to talk to salesmen. (*Pause.*) They're *lonely*, something. (*Pause.*) They like to feel *superior*, I don't know. Never bought a fucking thing. You're sitting down 'The Rio Rancho *this*, the blah blah blah,' 'The Mountain View,' 'Oh yes. My brother told me that . . .' They got a grapevine. Fuckin' Indians, George. Not my cup of tea. Speaking of which I want to tell you something: (*Pause.*) I never got a cup of tea with them. You see them in the restaurants. A supercilious race. What is this *look* on their face all the time? I don't know. (*Pause.*) I don't know. Their broads all look like they just got fucked with a dead *cat, I* don't know. (*Pause.*) I don't know. I don't like it. Christ . . .

AARONOW. What?

MOSS. The whole fuckin' thing . . . The pressure's just too great. You're ab . . . you're absolu . . . they're too important. All of them. You go in the door. I . . . 'I got to *close* this fucker, or I don't eat lunch.' 'Or I don't win the *Cadillac* . . .' . . .we fuckin' work too hard. You work too hard. We all, I remember when we were at Platt . . . huh? Glen Ross Farms . . . *didn't* we sell a bunch of that . . .?

AARONOW. They came in and they, you know . . .

MOSS. Well, they fucked it up.

AARONOW. They did.

MOSS. They killed the goose.

AARONOW. They did.

MOSS. And now . . .

AARONOW. We're stuck with *this* . . .

MOSS. We're stuck with *this* fucking shit . . .

AARONOW. . . . *this* shit . . .

MOSS. It's too . . .

AARONOW. It is.

MOSS. Eh?

AARONOW. It's too . . .

MOSS. You get a bad month, all of a . . .

AARONOW. You're on this . . .

MOSS. All of, they got you on this 'board . . .'

AARONOW. I, I . . . I . . .

MOSS. Some *contest* board . . .

AARONOW. I . . .

MOSS. It's not right.

AARONOW. It's not.

MOSS. No.

   Pause.

AARONOW. And it's not right to the *customers.*

MOSS. I know it's not. I'll tell you, you got, you know, you got
. . . what did I learn as a kid on Western? Don't sell a guy one
car. Sell him *five* cars over fifteen years.

AARONOW. That's right?

MOSS. Eh . . .?

AARONOW. That's right?

MOSS. Goddam right, that's right. Guys come on: 'Oh, the blah
blah blah, *I* know what I'll do: I'll go in and rob everyone
blind and go to Argentina cause nobody even *thought* of this
before.'

AARONOW. . . . that's right . . .

MOSS. Eh?

AARONOW. No. That's absolutely right.

MOSS. And so they kill the goose, I, I, I'll . . . and a fuckin'
man, worked all his *life* has got to . . .

AARONOW. . . . that's right . . .

MOSS. Cower in his *boots.*

AARONOW (*simultaneously with 'boots'*). Shoes, Boots, yes . . .

MOSS. For some fuckin' 'Sell ten thousand and you win the
steak knives . . .'

AARONOW. For some *sales* pro . . .

MOSS. . . . Sales promotion, 'you *lose,* then we fire your'
. . . No. It's *medieval* . . . it's wrong. 'Or we're going to fire
your ass.' It's wrong.

AARONOW. Yes.

MOSS. Yes, it is. And you know who's responsible?

AARONOW. Who?

MOSS. You know who it is. It's Mitch. And Murray. Cause it
doesn't have to be this way.

AARONOW. No.

MOSS. Look at Jerry Graff. He's *clean,* he's doing business for
himself, he's got his, that *list* of his with the *nurses* . . . see?
You see? That's *thinking.* Why take ten per cent? A ten per
cent comm . . . why are we giving the rest away? What are we
giving ninety per . . . for *nothing.* For some jerk sit in the
office tell you 'Get out there and close.' 'Go win the
Cadillac.' Graff. He goes out and *buys.* He pays top dollar for
the . . . you see?

AARONOW. Yes.

MOSS. That's *thinking.* Now, he's got the leads, he goes in
business for *himself.* He's . . . that's what I . . . that's
thinking! 'Who? Who's got a steady *job,* a couple bucks
nobody's touched, who?'

AARONOW. Nurses.

MOSS. So Graff buys a fucking list of nurses, one grand — if he
paid two I'll eat my hat — four, five thousand nurses, and

he's going *wild* . . .

AARONOW. . . . he is?

MOSS. He's doing *very* well.

AARONOW. I heard that they were running cold.

MOSS. The nurses?

AARONOW. Yes.

MOSS. You hear a *lot* of things . . . He's doing very well. He's doing *very* well.

AARONOW. With River Oaks?

MOSS. River Oaks, Brook Farms. *All* of that shit. Somebody told me, you know what he's clearing *himself*? Fourteen, fifteen grand a *week*.

AARONOW. Himself?

MOSS. That's what I'm *saying*. Why? The *leads*. He's got the good leads . . . what are we, we're sitting in the shit here. Why? We have to go to *them* to *get* them. Huh. Ninety per cent our sale, we're *paying* to the *office* for the *leads*.

AARONOW. The leads, the overhead, the telephones, there's *lots* of things.

MOSS. What do you need? A *telephone*, some broad to say 'Good morning,' nothing . . . nothing . . .

AARONOW. No, it's not that simple, Dave . . .

MOSS. *Yes*. It *is*. It *is* simple, and you know what the hard part is?

AARONOW. What?

MOSS. Starting up.

AARONOW. What hard part?

MOSS. Of doing the thing. The dif . . . the difference. Between me and Jerry Graff. Going to business for yourself. The hard part is . . . you know what it is?

AARONOW. What?

MOSS. Just the *act*.

AARONOW. What act?

MOSS. To say 'I'm going on my own.' Cause what you do, George, let me tell you what you do: you find yourself in *thrall* to someone else. And we *enslave* ourselves. To *please*. To win some fucking *toaster* . . . to . . . to . . . and the guy who got there first made *up* those . . .

AARONOW. . . . that's right . . .

MOSS. He made *up* those rules, and we're working for *him*.

AARONOW. That's the truth . . .

MOSS. That's the *god's* truth. And it gets me depressed. I *swear* that it does. At MY AGE. To see a goddam: 'Somebody wins the Cadillac this month. P.S. Two guys get fucked.'

AARONOW. *Huh*.

MOSS. You don't *axe* your sales force.

AARONOW. No.

MOSS. You . . .

AARONOW. You . . .

MOSS. You *build* it!

AARONOW. That's what I . . .

MOSS. You fucking *build* it! Men come . . .

AARONOW. Men come *work* for you . . .

MOSS. . . . you're absolutely right.

AARONOW. They . . .

MOSS. They have . . .

AARONOW. When they . . .

MOSS. Look look look look, when they *build* your business, then you can't fucking turn around, *enslave* them, treat them like *children,* fuck them up the ass, leave them to fend for themselves . . . no. (*Pause.*) No. (*Pause.*) You're absolutely right, and I want to tell you something.

AARONOW. What?

MOSS. I want to tell you what somebody should do.

AARONOW. What?

MOSS. Someone should stand up and strike *back*.

AARONOW. What do you mean?

MOSS. *Somebody* . . .

AARONOW. Yes . . .?

MOSS. Should do something to *them*.

AARONOW. What?

MOSS. Something. To pay them back.

>   *Pause.*

>   Someone, someone should hurt them. Murray and Mitch.

AARONOW. Someone should hurt them.

MOSS. Yes.

>   *Pause.*

AARONOW. How?

MOSS. How? Do something to hurt them. Where they live.

AARONOW. What?

>   *Pause.*

MOSS. Someone should rob the office.

AARONOW. Huh.

MOSS. That's what I'm *saying*. We were, if we were that kind of guys, to knock it off, and *trash* the joint, it looks like robbery, and *take* the fuckin' leads out of the files . . . go to Jerry Graff.

>   *Long pause.*

AARONOW. What could we get for them?

MOSS. What could we *get* for them? I don't know. Buck a *throw* . . . buck-a-half a throw . . . I don't know . . . Hey, who knows what they're worth, what do they *pay* for them? All told . . . must be, I'd . . . three bucks a throw . . . *I* don't know.

AARONOW. How many leads have we got?

MOSS. The *Glengarry* . . . the premium leads . . .? I'd say we got five thousand. Five. Five thousand leads.

AARONOW. And you're saying a fella could take and sell these leads to Jerry Graff.

MOSS. Yes.

AARONOW. How do you know he'd buy them?

MOSS. Graff? Because I worked for him.

AARONOW. You haven't talked to him.

MOSS. No. What do you mean? Have I talked to him about *this*?

Pause.

AARONOW. Yes. I mean are you actually *talking* about this, or are we just . . .

MOSS. No, we're just . . .

AARONOW. We're just *'talking'* about it.

MOSS. We're just *speaking* about it. (*Pause.*) As an *idea*.

AARONOW. As an idea.

MOSS. Yes.

AARONOW. We're not actually *talking* about it.

MOSS. No.

AARONOW. Talking about it as a . . .

MOSS. *No.*

AARONOW. As a *robbery*.

MOSS. As a 'robbery'?! No.

AARONOW. *Well.* Well . . .

MOSS. *Hey.*

Pause.

AARONOW. So all this, um, you didn't, actually, you didn't actually go talk to Graff.

MOSS. Not actually, no.

Pause.

AARONOW. You didn't?

MOSS. No. Not actually.

AARONOW. Did you?

MOSS. What did I say?

AARONOW. What did you say?

MOSS. Yes. (*Pause.*) I said 'Not actually'. The fuck you care, George? We're just *talking* . . .

AARONOW. We are?

MOSS. Yes.

Pause.

AARONOW. Because, because, you know, it's a *crime*.

MOSS. That's right. It's a crime. It is a crime. It's also very safe.

AARONOW. You're actually *talking* about this?

MOSS. That's right.

Pause.

AARONOW. You're going to steal the leads?

MOSS. Have I said that?

Pause.

AARONOW. Are you?

Pause.

MOSS. Did I say that?

AARONOW. Did you talk to Graff?

MOSS. Is that what I said?

AARONOW. What did he say?

MOSS. What did he say? He'd *buy* them.

Pause.

AARONOW. You're going to steal the leads and sell the leads to him?

Pause.

MOSS. Yes.

AARONOW. What will he pay?

MOSS. A buck a shot.

AARONOW. For five thousand?

MOSS. However they are, that's the deal. A buck a throw. Five thousand dollars. Split it half and half.

AARONOW. You're saying 'me'.

MOSS. Yes. (*Pause.*) Twenty-five hundred apiece. One night's work, and the job with Graff. Working the premium leads.

Pause.

AARONOW. A job with Graff.

MOSS. Is that what I said?

AARONOW. He'd give me a job.

MOSS. He would take you on. Yes.

Pause.

AARONOW. Is that the truth?

MOSS. Yes. It is, George. (*Pause.*) Yes. It's a big decision. (*Pause.*) And it's a big reward. (*Pause.*) It's a big reward. For one night's work. (*Pause.*) But it's got to be tonight.

AARONOW. What?

MOSS. What? What? The *leads*.

AARONOW. You have to steal the leads tonight?

MOSS. That's *right,* the guys are moving them down-town. After the thirtieth. Murray and Mitch. After the contest.

AARONOW. You're, you're saying so you have to go in there tonight and . . .

MOSS. *You . . .*

AARONOW. I'm sorry?

MOSS. *You.*

Pause.

AARONOW. Me?

MOSS. *You* have to go in. (*Pause.*) *You* have to get the leads.

Pause.

AARONOW. I do?

MOSS. Yes.

AARONOW. I . . .

MOSS. It's not something for nothing, George, I took you in on this, you have to go. That's your thing. I've made the deal with Graff. I can't go. I can't go in, I've spoken on this too much. I've got a big mouth. (*Pause.*) 'The fucking leads' et cetera, blah blah blah '. . . the fucking tight ass company . . .'

AARONOW. They'll know when you go over to Graff . . .

MOSS. What will they know? That I stole the leads? I *didn't* steal the leads, I'm going to the *movies* tonight with a friend, and then I'm going to the Como Inn. Why did I go to Graff? I got a better deal. *Period.* Let 'em prove something. They can't prove anything that's not the case.

Pause.

AARONOW. *Dave.*

MOSS. Yes.

AARONOW. You want me to break into the office tonight and steal the leads?

MOSS. Yes.

Pause.

AARONOW. No.

MOSS. Oh, yes, George.

AARONOW. What does that mean?

MOSS. Listen to this. I have an alibi, I'm going to the Como Inn, why? Why? The place gets robbed, they're going to come looking for *me*. Why? Because I probably did it. Are you going to turn me in? (*Pause.*) George? Are you going to turn me in?

AARONOW. What if you don't get caught?

MOSS. They come to you, you going to turn me in?

AARONOW. Why would they come to me?

MOSS. They're going to come to *everyone*.

AARONOW. Why would I *do* it?

MOSS. You wouldn't, George, that's why I'm talking to you.
  Answer me. They come to you. You going to turn me in?

AARONOW. No.

MOSS. Are you sure?

AARONOW. Yes. I'm sure.

MOSS. Then listen to this: I have to get those leads tonight.
  That's something I have to do. If I'm not at the *movies* . . . if
  I'm not eating over at the Inn . . . If you don't do this, then *I*
  have to come in here . . .

AARONOW. . . . you don't have to come in.

MOSS. . . . and *rob* the place . . .

AARONOW. . . . I thought that we were only talking . . .

MOSS. . . . they *take* me, then. They're going to ask me who
  were my accomplices.

AARONOW. *Me?*

MOSS. Absolutely.

AARONOW. That's ridiculous.

MOSS. Well, to the law, you're an accessory. Before the fact.

AARONOW. I didn't ask to be.

MOSS. Then tough luck, George, because you are.

AARONOW. Why? *Why,* because you only *told* me about it?

MOSS. That's right.

AARONOW. Why are you doing this to me, Dave? Why are you
  talking this way to me? I don't understand. Why are you
  doing this at *all* . . .?

MOSS. That's none of your fucking business . . .

AARONOW. Well, well, well, *talk* to me, we sat down to eat *dinner,* and here I'm a *criminal* . . .

MOSS. You *went* for it.

AARONOW. In the abstract . . .

MOSS. So I'm making it concrete.

AARONOW. Why?

MOSS. Why? Why *you* going to give me five grand?

AARONOW. Do you need five grand?

MOSS. Is that what I just said?

AARONOW. You need money? Is that the . . .

MOSS. Hey, hey, let's just keep it simple, what I need is not the . . . what do *you* need . . .?

AARONOW. What is the five grand? (*Pause.*) What is the, you said that we were going to *split* five . . .

MOSS. I lied. (*Pause.*) Alright? My end is *my* business. Your end's twenty-five. In or out. You tell me, you're out you take the consequences.

AARONOW. I do?

MOSS. Yes.

Pause.

AARONOW. And why is that?

MOSS. Because you listened.

Scene Three

The restaurant. ROMA is seated alone at the booth. LINGK is at the booth next to him. ROMA is talking to him.

ROMA. . . . all train compartments smell vaguely of shit. It gets so you don't mind it. That's the worst thing that I can confess. You know how long it took me to get there? A long time. When you *die* you're going to regret the things you don't

do. You think you're *queer* . . .? I'm going to tell you
something: we're *all* queer. You think that you're a *thief*?
So *what*? You get befuddled by a middle-class morality . . .?
Get *shut* of it. Shut it out. You cheated on your wife . . .?
You *did* it, *live* with it. (*Pause.*) You fuck little girls, so
be it. There's an absolute morality? May *be*. And *then* what?
If you *think* there is, then *be* that thing. Bad people go to
hell? I don't *think* so. If you think that, act that way. A hell
exists on earth? Yes. I won't live in it. That's *me*. You ever
take a dump made you feel you'd just slept for twelve
hours . . .?

LINGK. Did I . . .?

ROMA. Yes.

LINGK. I don't know.

ROMA. Or a *piss* . . .? A great meal fades in reflection.
Everything else gains. You know why? Cause it's only food.
This shit we eat, it keeps us going. But it's only food. The
great fucks that you may have had. What do you remember
about them?

LINGK. What do I . . .?

ROMA. Yes.

LINGK. Mmmm . . .?

ROMA. I don't know. For *me,* I'm saying, what it is, it's
probably not the orgasm. Some broads, forearms on your
neck, something her *eyes* did. There was a *sound* she made
. . . or, me, lying, in the, I'll tell you: me lying in bed: the
next day she brought me *café au lait.* She gives me a
cigarette, my balls feel like concrete. Eh? What I'm saying,
What is our life: (*Pause.*) it's looking forward or it's looking
back. And that's our life. That's *it*. Where is the *moment*?
(*Pause.*) And what is it that we're afraid of? Loss. What else?
(*Pause.*) The *bank* closes. We get *sick,* my wife died on a
plane, the stock market collapsed . . . the house burnt down
. . . what of these happen . . .? None of 'em. We worry
anyway. What does this mean? I'm not *secure*. How can I be
secure? (*Pause.*) Through amassing wealth beyond all

measure? No. And what's beyond all measure? That's a sickness. That's a trap. There is no measure. Only greed. How can we act? The right way, we would say, to deal with this: 'there is a one-in-a-million chance that so and so will happen . . . *Fuck* it, it won't happen to *me*' . . . No. We know that's not right, I think, we say the correct way to deal with this is 'There is a one in so-and-so chance this will happen . . . God *protect* me. I am powerless, let it not happen to me . . .' But no to *that*. I say. There's something else. What is it? 'If it happens, AS IT MAY for that is not within our powers, I will *deal* with it, just as I do *today* with what draws my concern today.' I say *this* is how we must act. I do those things which seem correct to me *today*. I trust myself. And if security concerns me, I do that which *today* I think will make me secure. And every day I *do* that, when that day *arrives* that I need a reserve, a) odds are that I have it and, b) the *true* reserve that I have is the strength that I have of *acting each day* without fear. (*Pause.*) According to the dictates of my mind. (*Pause.*) Stocks, bonds, objects of art, real estate. Now: what are they? (*Pause.*) An opportunity. To what? To make money? Perhaps. To *lose* money? Perhaps. To 'indulge' and to 'learn' about ourselves? Perhaps. *So fucking what?* What *isn't?* They're an *opportunity*. That's all. They're an *event*. A guy comes up to you, you make a call, you send in a brochure, it doesn't matter, 'There these *properties* I'd like for you to see.' What does it mean? What you *want* it to mean. (*Pause.*) Money? (*Pause.*) If that's what it signifies to you. Security? (*Pause.*) Comfort? 'Some schmuck wants to make a buck on me'; or, 'I feel a vibration *fate* is calling' . . . all it is is THINGS THAT HAPPEN TO YOU. (*Pause.*) That's all it is. How are they different? (*Pause.*) Some poor newly married guy gets run down by a cab. Some *busboy* wins the lottery . . . (*Pause.*) All it is, it's a carnival. What's special . . . what *draws* us . . .? (*Pause.*) We're all different. (*Pause.*) We're not the same . . . (*Pause.*) We're not the same . . . (*Pause.*) Hmmm . . . (*Pause. Sighs.*) It's been a long day. (*Pause.*) What are you drinking?

LINGK. Gimlet.

ROMA. Well, let's have a couple more. My name is Richard
Roma, what's yours?

LINGK. Lingk. James Lingk.

ROMA. James. I'm glad to meet you. (*They shake hands.*) I'm
glad to meet you, James. (*Pause.*) I want to show you
something. (*Pause.*) It might mean *nothing* to you . . . and
it might not. I don't know. I don't know anymore. (*Pause.
He takes out a small map and spreads it on a table.*) What is
that? Florida. Glengarry Highlands. Florida. 'Florida.
Bullshit.' And maybe that's true; and that's what *I* said: but
look *here*: What is this? This is a piece of land. Listen to
what I'm going to tell you now:

Act Two

ACT TWO

The Real Estate Office. Ransacked. A broken plate glass window boarded up, glass all over the floor. AARONOW *and* WILLIAMSON *standing around, smoking.*

Pause.

AARONOW. People used to say that there are numbers of such magnitude that multiplying them by two made no difference.

Pause.

WILLIAMSON. Who used to say that?

AARONOW. In school.

Pause.

BAYLEN, *a detective, comes out of the inner office.*

BAYLEN. Alright . . .?

ROMA *enters from the street.*

ROMA. *Williamson . . . Williamson,* they stole the *contracts . . .?*

BAYLEN. Excuse me, sir . . .

ROMA. Did they get my contracts?

WILLIAMSON. They got . . .

BAYLEN. Excuse me, fella.

ROMA. . . . did they . . .

BAYLEN. Would you excuse us, please . . .?

ROMA. Don't *fuck* with me, fella. I'm talking about a fuckin' Cadillac car that you owe me . . .

WILLIAMSON. They didn't get your contract. I filed it before I left.

ROMA. They didn't get my contracts?

WILLIAMSON. They: excuse me . . . (*He goes back into the inner room with the detective.*)

ROMA. Oh, *fuck. Fuck.* (*He starts kicking the desk.*) FUCK FUCK FUCK! WILLIAMSON!!! WILLIAMSON!!! (*He goes to the door* WILLIAMSON *went into, tries the door, it's locked.*) OPEN THE FUCKING . . . WILLIAMSON . . .

BAYLEN (*coming out*). Who are you?

WILLIAMSON *comes out.*

WILLIAMSON. They didn't get the contracts.

ROMA. Did they . . .

WILLIAMSON. They got, listen to me . . .

ROMA. Th . . .

WILLIAMSON. Listen to me: they got *some* of them.

ROMA. Some of them . . .

BAYLEN. Who told you . . .?

ROMA. Who told me wh . . .? You've got a fuckin', you've . . . a . . . who is this . . .? You've got a *board-up* on the window . . . *Moss* told me.

BAYLEN (*looking back toward the inner office*). Moss . . . Who told him?

ROMA. How the fuck do *I* know? (*To* WILLIAMSON:) *What . . . talk* to me.

WILLIAMSON. They took *some* of the con . . .

ROMA. . . . some of the contracts . . . Lingk. James Lingk. I closed . . .

WILLIAMSON. You closed him yesterday.

ROMA. *Yes.*

WILLIAMSON. It went down. I filed it.

ROMA. You did?

WILLIAMSON. Yes.

ROMA. Then I'm over the fucking top and you owe me a Cadillac.

WILLIAMSON. I . . .

ROMA. And I don't want any fucking shit and I don't give a shit, Lingk puts me over the top, you filed it, that's fine, any other shit kicks out *you* go back. You . . . *you* reclose it, cause I *closed* it and you . . . you owe me the car.

BAYLEN. Would you excuse us, please.

AARONOW. I, um, and may, maybe they're in, they're in . . . you should, John, if we're ins . . .

WILLIAMSON. I'm sure that we're insured, George . . . (*Going back inside.*)

ROMA. Fuck insured. You owe me a car.

BAYLEN (*stepping back into his room*). Please don't leave. I'm going to talk to you. What's your name?

ROMA. Are you talking to me?

Pause.

BAYLEN. Yes.

Pause.

ROMA. My name is Richard Roma.

BAYLEN *goes back into the inner room.*

AARONOW. I, you know, they should be insured.

ROMA. What do *you* care . . .?

AARONOW. Then, you know, they wouldn't be so ups . . .

ROMA. Yeah. That's swell. Yes. You're right. (*Pause.*) How are you?

AARONOW. I'm fine. You mean the *board*? You mean the *board* . . .?

ROMA. I don't . . . yes. Okay, the board.

AARONOW. I'm, I'm, I'm, I'm fucked on the board. *You.* You see how . . . I . . . (*Pause.*) I can't . . . my mind must be in other places. Cause I can't do any . . .

ROMA. *What?* You can't do *what*?

Pause.

AARONOW. I can't close 'em.

ROMA. Well, they're old. I saw the shit that they were giving you.

AARONOW. Yes.

ROMA. Huh?

AARONOW. Yes. They are old.

ROMA. They're ancient.

AARONOW. Clear . . .

ROMA. Clear Meadows. That shit's dead.

Pause.

AARONOW. It *is* dead.

ROMA. It's a waste of time.

AARONOW. Yes. (*Long pause.*) I'm no fucking good.

ROMA. That's . . .

AARONOW. Everything I . . . *you* know . . .

ROMA. That's not . . . Fuck that shit, George. You're a, *hey,* you had a bad month. You're a good man, George.

AARONOW. I am?

ROMA. You hit a bad streak. We've all . . . look at this: fifteen units Mountain View, the fucking things get stole.

AARONOW. He said he filed . . .

ROMA. He filed half of them, he filed the *big* one. All the little one, I have, I have to go back and . . . ah *fuck,* I got to go out like a fucking schmuck hat in my hand and reclose the . . . (*Pause.*) I mean, talk about a fucking streak, that would sap *anyone's* self-confi . . . I got to go out and reclose all my . . . Where's the phones?

AARONOW. They stole . . .

ROMA. They stole the . . .

AARONOW. What. What kind of outfit are we running where . . . where anyone . . .

ROMA (*to himself*). They stole the phones.

AARONOW. Where *criminals* can come in here . . . they take the . . . They stole the phones.

ROMA. They stole the leads. They're . . . *Christ.* (*Pause.*) What am I going to do this month? Oh *shit* . . . (*He starts for the door.*)

AARONOW. You think they're going to catch . . . where are you going?

ROMA. Down the street.

WILLIAMSON *sticks his head out of the door.*

WILLIAMSON. Where are you going?

ROMA. To the restaura . . . what do you fucking . . . ?

WILLIAMSON. . . . aren't you going out today?

ROMA. With what? (*Pause.*) With what, John, they took the leads . . .

WILLIAMSON. I have the stuff from last year's . . .

ROMA. Oh. Oh. Oh your 'Nostalgia' file, that's fine. No. Swell. Cause I don't have to . . .

WILLIAMSON. . . . you want to go out today . . .?

ROMA. Cause I don't have to *eat* this month. No. Okay. *Give* 'em to me . . . (*To himself.*) Fucking Mitch and Murray going to shit a br . . . what am I going to *do* all . . .

WILLIAMSON *starts back into the office. He is accosted by* AARONOW.

AARONOW. Were the leads . . .

ROMA. . . . what am I going to *do* all month . . .?

AARONOW. Were the leads insured?

WILLIAMSON (*long suffering*). I don't know, George, why?

AARONOW. Cause, you know, cause they weren't, I know that Mitch and Murray uh . . .

Pause.

WILLIAMSON. What?

AARONOW. That they're going to be upset.

WILLIAMSON. That's right. (*Going back into his office. To* ROMA:)

You want to go out today . . .? (*Pause.*)

AARONOW. He said we're all going to have to go talk to the guy.

ROMA. What?

AARONOW. He said we . . .

ROMA. To the cop?

AARONOW. Yeah.

ROMA. Yeah. That's swell. *Another* waste of time.

AARONOW. A waste of time? Why?

ROMA. *Why*? Cause they aren't going to find the guy.

AARONOW. The cops?

ROMA. Yes. The cops. No.

AARONOW. They aren't?

ROMA. No.

AARONOW. Why don't you think so?

ROMA. Why? Because they're *stupid.* 'Where were you last night . . .?'

AARONOW. Where were you?

ROMA. Where was *I*?

AARONOW. Yes.

ROMA. I was at home, where were *you*?

AARONOW. At home.

ROMA. *See* . . .? Were you the guy who broke in?

AARONOW. Was I?

ROMA. Yes.

AARONOW. No.

ROMA. Then don't sweat it, George, you know why?

AARONOW. No.

ROMA. You have nothing to hide.

AARONOW (*pause*). When I talk to the police, I get nervous.

ROMA. Yeah. You know who doesn't?

AARONOW. No, who?

ROMA. Thieves.

AARONOW. Why?

ROMA. They're inured to it.

AARONOW. You think so?

ROMA. Yes.

Pause.

AARONOW. But what should I *tell* them?

ROMA. The truth, George. Always tell the truth. It's the easiest thing to remember.

WILLIAMSON *comes out of the office with leads.* ROMA *takes one, reads it.*

ROMA. *Patel*? Ravidam *Patel*? How am I going to make a living on these deadbeat *wogs*? Where did you get this, from the *morgue*?

WILLIAMSON. If you don't want it, give it back.

ROMA. I don't 'want' it, if you catch my drift.

WILLIAMSON. I'm giving you *three* leads. You . . .

ROMA. What's the fucking point in *any* case . . .? What's the *point*? I got to argue with *you*, I got to knock heads with the *cops*, I'm busting my *balls*, sell your *dirt* to fucking *deadbeats* money in the *mattress*, I come back you can't even manage to keep the contracts safe, I have to go back and close them *again* . . . what the fuck am I wasting my time, fuck this shit. I'm going out and reclose last week's stuff . . .

WILLIAMSON. Don't do it, they might find him.

ROMA. They might find the guy?

WILLIAMSON. Yes.

ROMA. Your 'source' tells you that?

WILLIAMSON. The word from Murray is: leave them alone. If we have to get a new sig he'll go out himself, he'll be the *President*, just come *in*, from out of *town* . . .

ROMA. Okay, okay, okay, gimme this shit. Fine. (*He takes the leads.*)

WILLIAMSON. I'm giving you three . . .

ROMA. Three? I count *two*.

WILLIAMSON. Three.

ROMA. Patel? Fuck *you*. Fuckin' *Shiva* handed him a million dollars, told him 'sign the deal', he wouldn't sign. And Vishnu, too. Into the bargain. Fuck *that*, John. You know your business, I know mine. Your business is being an *asshole*, and I find out whose fucking *cousin* you are, I'm going to go to him and figure out a way to have your *ass* . . . fuck you — I'll wait for the new leads.

SHELLY LEVENE *enters*.

LEVENE. Get the *chalk*. Get the *chalk* . . . get the *chalk*! I closed 'em! I *closed* the cocksucker. Get the chalk and put me on the *board*. I'm going to Hawaii! Put me on the Cadillac board, Williamson! Pick up the fuckin' chalk. Eight units. Mountain View . . .

ROMA. You sold eight Mountain View?

LEVENE. You bet your ass. Who wants to go to lunch? Who wants to go to lunch? I'm buying. (*He slaps a contract down on* WILLIAMSON's *desk.*) Eighty-two fucking grand. And twelve grand in commission. John. (*Pause.*) On fucking deadbeat magazine subscription leads.

WILLIAMSON. Who?

LEVENE (*pointing to the contract*). *Read* it. Bruce and Harriett Nyborg. (*Looking around.*) What happened here?

AARONOW. Fuck. I had them on River Glen.

LEVENE *looks around.*

LEVENE. What happened?

WILLIAMSON. Somebody broke in.

ROMA. Eight units?

LEVENE. That's right.

ROMA. *Shelly* . . .!

LEVENE. Hey, big fucking deal. Broke a bad streak . . .

AARONOW. Shelly, the Machine, Levene.

LEVENE. You . . .

AARONOW. That's great.

LEVENE. Thank you, George.

> BAYLEN *sticks his head out of the room, calls in 'Aaronow'.*
> AARONOW *goes into the side room.*

Get on the phone, call Mitch . . .

ROMA. They took the phones . . .

LEVENE. They . . .

BAYLEN. *Aaronow* . . .

ROMA. They took the typewriters, they took the leads, they took the *cash,* they took the *contracts* . . .

LEVENE. Wh . . . wh . . . Wha . . .?

AARONOW. We had a robbery.

> *Pause.*

LEVENE. When?

ROMA. Last night, this morning . . .

> *Pause.*

LEVENE. They took the leads?

ROMA. Mmm.

> MOSS *comes out of the interrogation.*

MOSS. Fuckin' asshole.

ROMA. What, they beat you with a rubber bat?

MOSS. Cop couldn't find his dick two hands and a map. Anyone talks to this guy's an *asshole* . . .

ROMA. You going to turn States?

MOSS. Fuck you, Ricky. I ain't going out today. I'm going home. I'm going home because nothing's *accomplished* here . . . Anyone *talks* to this guy is . . .

ROMA. Guess what the Machine did?

MOSS. Fuck the Machine.

ROMA. Mountain View. Eight units.

MOSS. Fuckin' cop's got no right talk to me that way. I didn't rob the place . . .

ROMA. You hear what I said?

MOSS. Yeah. He closed a deal.

ROMA. Eight units. Mountain View.

MOSS (*To* LEVENE). You did that?

LEVENE. Yeah.

   Pause.

MOSS. Fuck you.

ROMA. Guess who?

MOSS. When . . .

LEVENE. Just now.

ROMA. Guess who?

MOSS. You just this morning . . .

ROMA. Harriett and blah blah Nyborg.

MOSS. You did that?

LEVENE. Eighty-two thousand dollars.

   Pause.

MOSS. Those fuckin' *deadbeats* . . .

LEVENE. My ass. I told 'em (*To* ROMA:) Listen to this: I said . . .

MOSS. Hey, I don't want to hear your fucking war stories . . .

ROMA. Fuck *you*, Dave . . .

LEVENE. 'You have to believe in your*self* . . . you,' look, 'alright . . .?'

MOSS (*to* WILLIAMSON). Give me some leads. I'm going out . . . I'm getting out of . . .

LEVENE. '. . . you have to believe in your*self* . . .'

MOSS. Na, fuck the leads, I'm going home.

LEVENE. 'Bruce, Harriett . . . Fuck *me*, believe in your*self* . . .'

ROMA. . . . we haven't got a lead . . .

MOSS. Why not?

ROMA. They took 'em . . .

MOSS. Hey, they're fuckin' garbage any case . . . This whole goddam . . .

LEVENE. '. . . You look around, you say "this one has so-and-so, and I have nothing" . . .'

MOSS. *Shit*.

LEVENE. '*Why*? Why don't I get the opportunities . . .?'

MOSS. And did they steal the contracts . . .?

ROMA. Fuck *you* care . . .?

LEVENE. 'I want to tell you something, Harriett . . .'

MOSS. . . . the fuck is *that* supposed to mean . . .?

LEVENE Will you shut up, I'm telling you this . . .

AARONOW *sticks his head out.*

AARONOW. Can we get some coffee . . .?

MOSS. How ya doing?

Pause.

AARONOW. Fine.

MOSS. Uh huh.

AARONOW. If anyone's going, I could use some coffee.

LEVENE. 'You *do* get the . . .' (*To* ROMA:) Huh? Huh?

MOSS. *Fuck* is that supposed to mean?

LEVENE. 'You *do* get the opportunity . . . You *get* them. As *I* do, as *anyone* does . . .'

MOSS. Ricky? . . . That I don't care they stole the contracts? (*Pause.*)

LEVENE. I got 'em in the kitchen. I'm eating her crumb cake.

MOSS. What does that mean?

ROMA. It *means,* Dave, you haven't closed a good one in a month, none of my business, you want to push me to answer you. (*Pause.*) And so you haven't got a contract to get stolen or so forth.

MOSS. You have a mean streak in you, Ricky, you know that . . .

LEVENE. Rick. Let me tell you. Wait, we're in the . . .

MOSS. Shut the fuck up. (*Pause.*) Ricky. You have a mean streak in you . . .(*To* LEVENE:) And what the fuck are *you* babbling about . . .? (*To* ROMA:) Bring that shit up. Of my volume. You were on a bad one and I brought it up to *you* you'd harbor it. (*Pause.*) You'd harbor it a long long while. And you'd be right.

ROMA. Who said 'Fuck the Machine'?

MOSS. '*Fuck the Machine*'? '*Fuck the Machine*'? What is this? *Courtesy* class . . .? You're *fucked,* Rick — are you fucking *nuts*? You're hot, so you think you're the *ruler* of this place . . .?! You want to . . .

LEVENE. Dave . . .

MOSS. . . . Shut up. Decide who should be dealt with how? Is that the thing? I come into the fuckin' office today, I get humiliated by some jagoff cop. I get accused of . . . I get this *shit* thrown in my face by you, you genuine shit, because you're top name on the board . . .

ROMA. Is that what I did? Dave? I humiliated you? My *God* . . . I'm *sorry* . . .

MOSS. Sittin' on top of the *world,* sittin' on top of the *world,* everything's fucking *peach*fuzz . . .

ROMA. Oh, and I don't get a moment to spare for a bust-out
humanitarian down on his luck lately. Fuck *you*, Dave, you
know you got a big *mouth*, and *you* make a close the whole
place stinks with your *farts* for a week. 'How much you just
ingested,' what a big *man* you are, 'Hey, let me buy you a
pack of gum. I'll show you how to *chew* it.' Your *pal* closes,
all that comes out of your mouth is *bile*, how fucked *up* you
are . . .

MOSS. *Who's* my pal . . .? And what are you, Ricky, huh, what
are you, Bishop *Sheean*? Who the fuck are *you*, Mr Slick . . .?
What are you, friend to the *workingman*? Big deal. Fuck *you*,
you got the memory a fuckin' *fly*. I never liked you.

ROMA. What is this, your farewell speech?

MOSS. I'm going home.

ROMA. Your farewell to the troops?

MOSS. I'm not going home. I'm going to Wis*con*sin.

ROMA. Have a good trip.

MOSS. Fuck you. Fuck the *lot* of you. Fuck you *all*.

MOSS *exits. Pause.*

ROMA (*to* LEVENE). You were saying? (*Pause.*) Come on.
Come on, you got them in the kitchen, you got the stats
spread out, you're in your shirtsleeves, you can *smell* it.
Huh? Snap out of it, you're eating her *crumb* cake.

Pause.

LEVENE. I'm eating her *crumb* cake . . .

ROMA. . . . how was it . . .?

LEVENE. From the store.

ROMA. . . . fuck *her* . . .

LEVENE. 'What we have to do is *admit* to ourself that we see
that opportunity . . . and *take* it. (*Pause.*) And that's it.' And
we *sit* there . . . (*Pause.*) I got the pen out . . .

ROMA. Always Be Closing . . .

LEVENE. That's what I'm *saying*. The *old* ways. The *old*

ways . . . convert the mother fucker . . . *sell* him . . . *sell* him . . . *make him sign the check.* (*Pause.*) The . . . Bruce, Harriett . . . the kitchen, blah: They got their money in *government* bonds . . . I say *fuck* it, we're going to go the whole route. I plat it out eight units. Eighty-two grand. I tell them. 'This is now. This is that *thing* that you've been dreaming of, you're going to find that suitcase on the train, the guy comes in the door, the bag that's full of money. This is it, *Harriett . . .*'

ROMA (*reflectively*). Harriett . . .

LEVENE. *Bruce* . . . 'I don't want to fuck *around* with you. I don't want to go *round* this, and *pussyfoot* around the thing, you have to look back on this. I do, too. I came here to do good for you and me. For *both* of us. Why take an interim position? *The only arrangement I'll accept* is full investment. Period. The whole eight units. I know that you're saying 'be safe,' I know what you're saying. I know if I left you to yourselves, you'd say 'come back tomorrow' and when I walked out that door, you'd make a cup of *coffee* . . . you'd sit *down* . . . and you'd think 'let's be safe . . .' and not to disappoint me you'd go *one* unit or maybe two, because you'd become scared because you'd met possi*bi*lity. But this won't do, and that's not the subject . . .' Listen to this, I actually said this: 'That's not the subject of our *evening* together.' Now I handed them the pen. I held it in my hand. I turned the contract eight units eighty-two grand. 'Now I want you to sign.' (*Pause.*) I sat there. Five minutes. Then, I sat there, Ricky, *twenty-two minutes* by the kitchen *clock*. (*Pause.*) Twenty-two minutes by the kitchen clock. Not a *word*, not a *motion*. What am I thinking? 'My arm's getting tired'? *No.* I *did* it. I *did* it. Like in the *old* days, Ricky. Like I was taught . . . Like, like, like I *used* to do . . . I did it.

ROMA. Like you taught me . . .

LEVENE. Bullshit, you're . . . No. That's raw . . . well, if I *did*, then I'm *glad* I did. I, *well.* I locked on them. All on them, nothing on me. All my thoughts are on them. I'm holding the last thought that I spoke: 'Now is the time.' (*Pause.*) They signed, Ricky. It was *great.* It was fucking great. It was like they wilted all at once. No *gesture* . . . nothing. Like together.

They, I swear to God, they both kind of *imperceptibly
slumped*. And he reaches and takes the pen and signs, he
passes it to her, she signs. It was so fucking solemn. I just let
it sit. I nod like this. I nod again. I grasp his hands. I shake
his hands. I grasp *her* hands. I nod at her like this. 'Bruce . . .
Harriett . . .' I'm beaming at them. I'm nodding like this. I
point back in the living-room, back to the sideboard. (*Pause.*)
I didn't fucking know there was a sideboard there!! He goes
back, he brings us a drink. Little shotglasses. A pattern in
'em. And we toast. In silence.

Pause.

ROMA. That was a great sale, Shelly.

Pause.

LEVENE. . . . Ah fuck.

WILLIAMSON *sticks his head out of the office.*

Leads! Leads! Williamson! Send me *out*! Send me *out*!

WILLIAMSON. The leads are coming.

LEVENE. *Get* 'em to me!

WILLIAMSON. I talked to Murray and Mitch an hour ago.
They're coming in, you understand they're a bit *upset* over
this morning's . . .

LEVENE. Did you tell 'em my sale?

WILLIAMSON. How could I tell 'em your sale? Eh? I don't
have a tel . . . I'll tell 'em your sale when they bring in the
leads. Alright? Shelly. Alright? We had a little . . . You closed
a deal. You made a good sale. Fine

LEVENE. It's better than a good sale. It's a . . .

WILLIAMSON. Look: I have a lot of things on my mind,
they're coming in, alright, they're very upset, I'm trying to
make some *sense* . . .

LEVENE. All that I'm *telling* you: that one thing you can tell
them it's a remarkable sale.

WILLIAMSON. The only thing remarkable is who you made it
to.

LEVENE. What does *that* fucking mean?

WILLIAMSON. That if the sale sticks, it will be a miracle.

LEVENE. Why should the sale not stick? Hey, fuck *you*. That's
what I'm saying. You have no idea of your job. A man's his
job and you're *fucked* at yours. You hear what I'm saying
to you? Your 'end of month board' . . . You can't run an
office. I don't care. You don't know what it *is*, you don't
have the *sense*, you don't have the *balls*. You ever been on a
sit? *Ever*? Has this cocksucker ever been . . . you ever sit
down with a cust . . .

WILLIAMSON. I were you, I'd calm down, Shelly.

LEVENE. *Would* you? *Would* you . . .? Or you're gonna *what*,
fire me?

WILLIAMSON. It's not impossible.

LEVENE. On an eighty-thousand dollar *day*? And it ain't even
noon.

ROMA. You closed 'em today?

LEVENE. Yes. I did. This *morning*. (*To* WILLIAMSON:) What
I'm *saying* to you: things can *change*. You *see*? This is where
you fuck *up*, because this is something you don't *know*. You
can't look down the *road*. And see what's *coming*. Might be
someone *else*, John. It might be someone *new*, eh? Someone
new. And you can't look *back*. Cause you don't know
history. You ask them. When we were at Rio Rancho, who
was top man? A month . . .? Two months . . .? Eight months
in twelve for three years in a row. You know what that
means? You know what that means? Is that *luck*? Is that
some, some, some purloined leads? That's *skill*. That's *talent*,
that's, that's . . .

ROMA. . . . *yes* . . .

LEVENE. . . . and you don't *remember*. Cause you weren't
around. That's cold *calling*. Walk up to the door. I don't even
know their *name*. I'm selling something they don't even *want*.
You talk about soft sell . . . before we had a name for it . . .
before we called it anything, we did it.

ROMA. That's right, Shel.

LEVENE. And, and, and, I *did* it. And I put a kid through
school. She . . . and . . . Cold *calling* fella. Door to door. But
you don't know. You don't know. You never heard of a
streak. You ever heard of 'marshalling your sales force' . . .
what are you, you're a *secretary,* John. Fuck *you.* That's my
message to you. Fuck you and kiss my ass. You don't like it,
I'll go talk to Jerry Graff. Period. Fuck you. Put me on the
board. And I want three worthwhile leads today and I don't
want any bullshit about them and I want 'em close together
cause I'm going to hit them all today. That's all I have to
say to you.

ROMA. He's right, Williamson.

WILLIAMSON *goes into a side office. Pause.*

LEVENE. It's not right. I'm sorry, and I'll tell you who's to
blame is Mitch and Murray.

ROMA *sees something outside the window.*

ROMA (*sotto*). Oh Christ.

LEVENE. The hell with him. We'll go to lunch, the leads won't
be up for . . .

ROMA. You're a client. I just sold you five waterfront
Glengarry Farms. I rub my head, throw me the cue
'Kenilworth'.

LEVENE. . . . What is it?

ROMA. Kenilw . . .

JAMES LINGK *enters the office.*

ROMA (*to* LEVENE). *I* own the property, my *mother* owns the
property, I put her *into* it. I'm going to show you on the
plats. You look when you get home A–3 through A–14 and
26 through 30. You take your time and if you still feel.

LEVENE. No, Mr Roma. I don't need the time, I've made a lot
of *investments* in the last . . .

LINGK. I've got to talk to you.

ROMA (*looking up*). Jim! What are you doing here? Jim Lingk,
D. Ray Morton . . .

LEVENE. Glad to meet you.

ROMA. I just put Jim into Black Creek . . . are you acquainted
with . . .

LEVENE. No . . . Black *Creek*. Yes. In *Florida*?

ROMA. Yes.

LEVENE. I wanted to *speak* with you about . . .

ROMA. Well, we'll do that this weekend.

LEVENE. My *wife* told me to look into . . .

ROMA. *Beautiful.* Beautiful rolling land. I was telling Jim and
Jinny, Ray, I want to tell you something. (*To* LEVENE:)
You, Ray, you eat in a lot of restaurants. I know you do . . .
(*To* LINGK:) Mr Morton's with American Express . . . he's
(*To* LEVENE:) I can tell Jim what you do . . .

LEVENE. Sure.

ROMA. Ray is Director of all European Sales and Services for
American Ex . . . (*To* LEVENE:) But I'm saying you haven't
had a *meal* until you've tasted . . . I was at the Lingks'
last . . . as a matter of fact, what was that Service Feature
you were talking about . . .

LEVENE. Which . . .

ROMA. 'Home Cooking' . . . what did you call it, you said it . . .
it was a tag phrase that you had . . .

LEVENE. Uh . . .

ROMA. Home . . .

LEVENE. Home cooking . . .

ROMA. The monthly interview . . .?

LEVENE. Oh! For the *magazine* . . .

ROMA. Yes. Is this something that I can talk ab . . .

LEVENE. Well, it isn't coming *out* until the February iss . . .
sure. Sure, go ahead, Rick.

ROMA. You're sure?

LEVENE (*nods*). Go ahead.

ROMA. Well, Ray was eating at one of his company's men's home in France . . . the man's French, isn't he?

LEVENE. No, his *wife* is.

ROMA. Ah. Ah, his wife is. Ray: what *time* do you have . . .?

LEVENE. Twelve fifteen.

ROMA. Oh! My God . . . I've got to get you on the *plane*!

LEVENE. Didn't I say I was taking the two o' . . .

ROMA. No. You said the One. That's why you said we couldn't talk till Kenilworth.

LEVENE. Oh, my God, you're right! I'm on the One . . . (*Getting up.*) Well, let's scoot . . .

LINGK. I've got to talk to you . . .

ROMA. I've got to get Ray to O'Hare . . .(*To* LEVENE:) Come on, let's hustle . . . (*Over his shoulder.*) John! Call American Express in *Pittsburgh* for Mr Morton, will you, tell them he's on the one o'clock. (*To* LINGK:) I'll see you . . . Christ, I'm sorry you came all the way in . . . I'm running Ray over to O'Hare . . . You wait here, I'll . . . no. (*To* LEVENE:) I'm meeting your man at the Bank . . . (*To* LINGK:) I wish you'd phoned . . . I'll tell you, wait: (*To* LINGK:) Are you and Jinny going to be home tonight? (*He rubs his forehead.*)

LINGK. I . . .

LEVENE. Rick.

ROMA. What?

LEVENE. *Kenilworth* . . .?

ROMA. I'm sorry . . .?

LEVENE. *Kenilworth.*

ROMA. Oh, God . . . Oh, God . . . (ROMA *takes* LINGK *aside, sotto:*) Jim, excuse me . . . Ray, I told you, who he is is *the* Senior Vice-President American Express. His family owns thirty-two per . . . Over the past years I've sold him . . . I can't tell you the dollar amount, but *quite* a lot of land. I promised five *weeks* ago that I'd go to the wife's birthday party in Kenilworth tonight. (*He sighs.*) I *have* to go. You understand. They treat me like a member of the family, so I have to go. It's funny, you know, you get a picture of the Corporation Type Company Man, all business . . . this man, *no.* We'll go out to his home sometime. Let's see. (*He checks his datebook.*) Tomorrow. No. Tomorrow, I'm in L.A. . . . *Monday* . . . I'll take you to lunch, where would you like to go?

LINGK. My wife . . .

ROMA *rubs his head.*

LEVENE (*standing in the door*). Rick . . .?

ROMA. I'm sorry, Jim. I can't talk now. I'll call you tonight . . . I'm sorry. I'm coming, Ray.

He starts for the door.

LINGK. My wife said I have to cancel the deal.

ROMA. It's a common reaction, Jim. I'll tell you what it is, and I know that that's why you married her. One of the reasons is *prudence.* It's a sizeable investment. One thinks *twice* . . . it's also something *women* have. It's just a reaction to the size of the investment. *Monday,* if you'd invite me for dinner again . . . (*To* LEVENE:) This woman can *cook* . . .

LEVENE (*simultaneously*). I'm sure she can . . .

ROMA (*to* LINGK). We're going to talk. I'm going to *tell* you something. Because (*Sotto:*) there's something about your acreage I want you to know. I can't talk about it now. I really shouldn't. And, in fact, by *law,* I . . . (*He shrugs, resigned.*) The man next to you, he bought his lot at forty-*two,* he phoned to say that he'd *already* had an offer . . . (ROMA *rubs his head.*)

LEVENE. Rick . . .?

ROMA. I'm coming, Ray . . . what a day! I'll call you this evening, Jim. I'm sorry you had to come in . . . Monday, lunch.

LINGK. My wife . . .

LEVENE. Rick, we really have to go.

LINGK. My wife . . .

ROMA. Monday.

LINGK. She called the Consumer . . . the Attorney, I don't know. The Attorney Gen . . . they said we have three days . . .

ROMA. *Who* did she call?

LINGK. I don't know, the Attorney Gen . . . the . . . some Consumer office, umm . . .

ROMA. Why did she do *that*, Jim?

LINGK. I don't know. (*Pause.*) They said we have three days. (*Pause.*) They said we have three days.

ROMA. Three days.

LINGK. To . . . you know. (*Pause.*)

ROMA. No I don't know. *Tell* me.

LINGK. To change our minds.

ROMA. Of *course* you have three days.

Pause.

LINGK. So we can't talk *Monday*.

Pause.

ROMA. Jim, Jim, you saw my book . . . I *can't, you* saw my book . . .

LINGK. But we have to *before* Monday. To get our money ba . . .

ROMA. Three *business* days. They mean three *business* days.

LINGK. Wednesday, Thursday, Friday.

ROMA. I don't understand.

LINGK. That's what they are. Three business . . . if I wait till Monday, my time limit runs out.

ROMA. You don't count Saturday.

LINGK. I'm not.

ROMA. No, I'm saying you don't include Saturday . . . in your three days. It's not a *business* day.

LINGK. But I'm not *counting* it. (*Pause.*) Wednesday. Thursday. Friday. So it would have elapsed.

ROMA. What would have elapsed?

LINGK. If we wait till Mon . . .

ROMA. When did you write the check?

LINGK. Yest . . .

ROMA. What was yesterday?

LINGK. Tuesday.

ROMA. And when was that check cashed?

LINGK. I don't know.

ROMA. What was the *earliest* it could have been cashed?

Pause.

LINGK. I don't know.

ROMA. *Today.* (*Pause.*) *Today.* Which, in any case, it was not, as there were a couple of points on the agreement I wanted to go over with you in any case.

LINGK. The check wasn't cashed?

ROMA. I just called down-town, and it's on their desk.

LEVENE. Rick . . .

ROMA. One moment, I'll be right with you. (*To* LINGK:) In fact, a . . . *one* point, which I spoke to you of which (*He looks around.*) I can't talk to you about here.

BAYLEN *puts his head out of the doorway.*

BAYLEN. Levene!!!

LINGK. I, I . . .

ROMA. Listen to me, the *statute,* it's for your protection. I have no complaints with that, in fact, I was a member of the board when we *drafted* it, so quite the *opposite.* It *says* that you can change your mind three working days from the time the deal is closed.

BAYLEN. Levene!

ROMA. Which, wait a second, which is not until the check is cashed.

BAYLEN. Levene!!

AARONOW *comes out of the* DETECTIVE's *office.*

AARONOW. I'm *through*, with *this* fucking mishagas. No one should talk to a man that way. How are you *talking* to me that . . .?

BAYLEN. Levene!

WILLIAMSON *puts his head out of the office.*

AARONOW. . . . how can you *talk* to me that . . . that . . .

LEVENE (*to* ROMA). Rick, I'm going to flag a cab.

AARONOW. *I* didn't rob . . .

WILLIAMSON *sees* LEVENE.

WILLIAMSON. Shelly: get in the office.

AARONOW. *I* didn't . . . why should *I* . . . 'Where were you last . . .' is anybody listening to me . . .? Where's Moss . . .? Where . . .?

BAYLEN. Levene? (*To* WILLIAMSON:) Is this Lev . . . (BAYLEN *accosting* LINGK.)

LEVENE (*taking* BAYLEN *into the office*). Ah. Ah. Perhaps I can advise you on that . . . (*To* ROMA *and* LINGK, *as he exits:*) *Excuse* us, will you . . .?

AARONOW (*simultaneous with* LEVENE's *speech above*). . . . Come in here . . . I *work* here, I don't come in here to be *mistreated* . . .

WILLIAMSON. Go to *lunch*, will you . . .

AARONOW. I want to *work* today, that's why I came . . .

WILLIAMSON. The leads come in, I'll let . . .

AARONOW. . . . that's why I came in. I thought I . . .

WILLIAMSON. Just go to lunch.

AARONOW. I don't *want* to go to lunch.

WILLIAMSON. Go to lunch, George.

AARONOW. Where does he get off to talk that way to a working man? It's not . . .

WILLIAMSON (*buttonholes him*). Will you take it outside, we have people trying to do *business* here . . .

AARONOW. That's what, that's what, that's what *I* was trying to do. (*Pause.*) That's why I came *in* . . . I meet *Gestapo* tac . . .

WILLIAMSON (*going back into his office*). Excuse me . . .

AARONOW. I meet *Gestapo* tactics . . . I meet *Gestapo* tactics . . . that's not right . . . No man has the right to . . . 'call an attorney,' that means you're guilt . . . you're under sus . . . 'Co', he says. 'Cooperate' or we'll go down-town. *That's* not . . . as long as I've . . .

WILLIAMSON (*bursting out of his office*). Will you get out of here? Will you get *out* of here? Will you? I'm trying to run an *office* here. Will you go to lunch? Go to lunch. Will you go to lunch? (*He retreats into his office.*)

ROMA (*to* AARONOW). Will you excuse . . .

AARONOW. Where did Moss . . .? I . . .

ROMA. Will you excuse us please?

AARONOW. Uh uh, did he go to the restaurant?

Pause. I . . . I . . . (*He exits.*)

ROMA. I'm *very* sorry, Jimmy. I apologise to you.

LINGK. It's not me, it's my wife.

ROMA (*pause*). What is?

LINGK. I told you.

ROMA. Tell me again.

LINGK. What's going on here?

ROMA. Tell me again. Your wife.

LINGK. I told you.

ROMA. You tell me again.

LINGK. She wants her money back.

ROMA. We're going to speak to her.

LINGK. No. She told me 'right now'.

ROMA. We'll speak to her, Jim . . .

LINGK. She won't listen.

  BAYLEN *sticks his head out.*

BAYLEN. *Roma.*

LINGK. She told me if not, I have to call the State's Attorney.

ROMA. No, no. That's just something she 'said'. We don't have to do that.

LINGK. She told me I *have* to.

ROMA. No, Jim.

LINGK. I *do.* If I don't get my *money* back . . .

  WILLIAMSON *points out* ROMA *to him.*

BAYLEN. Roma! (*To* ROMA:) I'm talking to you . . .

ROMA. I've . . . look. (*Generally.*) Will someone get this guy off my back.

BAYLEN. You have a problem?

ROMA. Yes, I have a problem. Yes, I *do,* my fr . . . It's not me that ripped the joint off, I'm doing *business.* I'll be with you in a *while.* You got it . . .? (*He looks back,* LINGK *is heading for the door.*) Where are you going?

LINGK. I'm . . .

ROMA. Where are you going . . .? This is *me* . . . This is Ricky, Jim. Jim, anything you *want,* you *want* it, you *have* it. You understand? This is *me.* Something *upset* you. Sit down, now sit down. You tell me what it is. (*Pause.*) Am I going to help you fix it? You're goddamned right I am. Sit down. Tell you something . . .? *Sometimes* we need someone from *outside.* It's . . . no, sit down . . . Now *talk* to me.

LINGK. I can't negotiate.

ROMA. What does that mean?

LINGK. That . . .

ROMA. . . . what, what, *say* it. Say it to me . . .

LINGK. I . . .

ROMA. What . . .?

LINGK. I . . .

ROMA. What . . .? Say the words.

LINGK. I don't have the *power*. (*Pause.*) I said it.

ROMA. What power?

LINGK. The power to negotiate.

ROMA. To negotiate what? (*Pause.*) To negotiate what?

LINGK. *This.*

ROMA. What, 'this'?

> *Pause.*

LINGK. The deal.

ROMA. The 'deal', *forget* the deal. *Forget* the deal, you've got something on your mind, Jim, what is it?

LINGK (*rising*). I can't talk to you, *you* met my wife, I . . .

> *Pause.*

ROMA. What? (*Pause.*) What? (*Pause.*) What, Jim: I tell you what, let's get out of here . . . let's go get a drink.

LINGK. She told me not to talk to you.

ROMA. Let's . . . no one's going to know, let's go around the *corner* and we'll get a drink.

LINGK. She told me I had to get back the check or call the State's Att . . .

ROMA. *Forget* the deal, Jimmy. (*Pause.*) *Forget* the deal . . .you know me. The deal's *dead*. Am I talking about the *deal*? That's *over*. Please. Let's talk about *you*. Come on. (*Pause.*

ROMA *rises and starts walking toward the front door.*) Come
on. (*Pause.*) Come on, Jim. (*Pause.*) I want to tell you
something. Your life is your own. You have a contract with
your wife. You have certain things you do *jointly,* you have a
bond there . . . and there are *other* things. Those things are
yours. You needn't feel *ashamed,* you needn't feel that
you're being *untrue* . . . or that she would abandon you if she
knew, this is your life. (*Pause.*) *Yes.* Now I want to *talk* to
you because you're obviously upset and that *concerns* me.
Now let's go. Right now.

LINGK *gets up and they start for the door.*

BAYLEN (*sticks his head out of the door*). Roma . . .

LINGK. . . . and . . . and . . .

Pause.

ROMA. What?

LINGK. And the check is . . .

ROMA. What did I *tell* you? (*Pause.*) What did I say about the
three days . . .?

BAYLEN. Roma, would you, I'd like to get some lunch . . .

ROMA. I'm talking with Mr Lingk. If you please, I'll be back in.
(*He checks his watch.*) I'll be back in a while . . . I told you,
check with Mr Williamson.

BAYLEN. The people down-town said . . .

ROMA. You call them again. Mr Williamson . . .!

WILLIAMSON. Yes.

ROMA. Mr Lingk and I are going to . . .

WILLIAMSON. Yes. Please. Please. (*To* LINGK:) The police
(*He shrugs.*) can be . . .

LINGK. What are the police doing?

ROMA. It's nothing . . .

LINGK. What are the *police* doing here . . .?

WILLIAMSON. We had a slight burglary last night.

ROMA. It was nothing . . . I was telling Mr Lingk . . .

WILLIAMSON. Mr Lingk. James Lingk. Your contract went
out. Nothing to . . .

ROMA. John . . .

WILLIAMSON. Your contract went out to the bank.

Pause.

LINGK. You cashed the check?

WILLIAMSON. We . . .

ROMA. . . . Mr Williamson . . .

WILLIAMSON. Your check was cashed yesterday afternoon.
And we're completely insured, as you know, in *any* case.
(*Pause.*)

LINGK (*to* ROMA). You cashed the check?

ROMA. Not to my knowledge, no . . .

WILLIAMSON. I'm sure we can . . .

LINGK. Oh, Christ . . . (*He starts out the door.*) Don't follow
me . . . Oh, Christ . . . (*Pause. To* ROMA:) I know I've let
you down. I'm sorry. For . . . Forgive . . . for . . . I don't
know anymore. (*Pause.*) Forgive me. (LINGK *exits.*)
(*Pause.*)

ROMA (*to* WILLIAMSON). You stupid fucking cunt. *You*,
Williamson . . . I'm talking to *you*, shithead . . . You just cost
me *six thousand dollars*. (*Pause.*) Six thousand dollars. And
one Cadillac. That's right. What are you going to do about it?
What are you going to do about it, asshole. You fucking *shit*.
Where did you learn your *trade*. You stupid fucking *cunt*.
You *idiot*. Whoever told you you could work with *men*?

BAYLEN. Could I . . .

ROMA. I'm going to have your *job,* shithead. I'm going
down-town and talk to Mitch and Murray, and I'm going to
Lemkin. I don't care *whose* nephew you are, who you know,
whose dick you're sucking on. You're going *out,* I swear to
you, you're going . . .

BAYLEN. Hey, fella, let's get this done . . .

ROMA. Anyone in this office lives on their *wits* . . . (*To*
BAYLEN:) I'm going to be with you in a second. (*To*
WILLIAMSON:) What you're hired for is to *help* us — does
that seem clear to you? To *help* us. *Not* to fuck us up . . . to
help *men* who are going *out* there to try to earn a *living*. You
fairy. You company man . . .I'll tell you something else. I
hope you knocked the joint off, I can tell our friend here
something might help him to catch you. (*He starts into the
room.*) You want to learn the first rule you'd know if you
ever spent a day in life, you never open your mouth till you
know what the shot is. (*Pause.*) You fuckin' *child* . . .
(LEVENE *has come out during the diatribe with* LINGK
and has sat at the back listening. To LEVENE:) Don't
leave. I have to talk to you. (*To* WILLIAMSON:) You
fucking *child* . . . (ROMA *goes into the inner room.*)

LEVENE. You *are* a shithead, Williamson . . . (*Pause.*)

WILLIAMSON. Mmm.

LEVENE. You can't think on your feet you should keep your
mouth closed. (*Pause.*) You hear me? I'm *talking* to you. Do
you hear me . . .?

WILLIAMSON. Yes. (*Pause.*) I hear you.

LEVENE. You can't learn that in an office. Eh? He's right. You
have to learn it on the streets. You can't *buy* that. You have
to *live* it.

WILLIAMSON. Mmm.

LEVENE. *Yes.* Mmm. *Yes. Precisely. Precisely.* Cause your
partner *depends* on it. (*Pause.*) I'm *talking* to you, I'm trying
to tell you something.

WILLIAMSON. You are?

LEVENE. Yes, I am.

WILLIAMSON. What are you trying to tell me?

LEVENE. What I was trying to tell you yesterday. Why you
don't belong in this business.

WILLIAMSON. Why I don't . . .

LEVENE. You listen to me, someday you might say, 'Hey . . .'

No, fuck that, you just listen what I'm going to say: Your
partner *depends* on you. Your partner . . . a man who's your
'partner' *depends* on you . . . you have to go *with* him and
for him . . . or you're shit, you're *shit*, you can't exist alone . . .

WILLIAMSON (*brushing past him*). Excuse me . . .

LEVENE. . . . excuse you, *nothing*, you be as cold as you want,
but you just fucked a good man out of six thousand dollars
and his goddam bonus cause you didn't know the *shot*, if
you can do that and you aren't man enough that it gets you,
then I don't know what, if you can't take *some thing* from
that . . . (*Blocking his way.*) you're *scum*, you're fucking
white-bread. You be as cold as you want. A *child* would
know it, he's right. (*Pause.*) You're going to make something
up, be sure it will *help* or keep your mouth closed.

Pause.

WILLIAMSON. Mmm.

LEVENE *lifts up his arm.*

LEVENE. Now I'm done with you.

Pause.

WILLIAMSON. How do you know I made it up?

LEVENE (*pause*). What?

WILLIAMSON. How do you know I made it up?

LEVENE. What are you talking about?

WILLIAMSON. You said 'You don't make something up unless
it's sure to help.' (*Pause.*) How did you know that I made it
up?

LEVENE. What are you talking about?

WILLIAMSON. I told the customer that his contract had gone
to the bank.

LEVENE. Well, hadn't it?

WILLIAMSON. No. (*Pause.*) It hadn't.

LEVENE. Don't *fuck* with me, John, don't *fuck* with me . . .
what are you saying?

WILLIAMSON. Well, I'm saying this, Shel: Usually I take the contracts to the bank. Last night I didn't. How did you know that? One night a year that I left a contract on my desk. Nobody knew that but *you.* Now how did you know that? (*Pause.*) You want to talk to me, you want to talk to someone *else* . . . because this is *my* job on the line, and you're going to *talk* to me: Now how did you know that contract was on my desk?

LEVENE. You're so full of shit.

WILLIAMSON. You robbed the office.

LEVENE (*laughs*). Sure!

WILLIAMSON. What'd you do with the leads? (*Pause. He points to the* DETECTIVE's *room.*) You want to go in there? I tell him what we know, he's going to dig up *something* . . . You got an alibi last night? You better have one. What did you do with the leads? If you tell me what you did with the leads, we can talk.

LEVENE. I don't know what you are saying.

WILLIAMSON. If you tell me where the leads are, I won't turn you in. If you *don't,* I am going to tell the cop you stole them, Mitch and Murray will see that you go to jail.

LEVENE. They wouldn't do that.

WILLIAMSON. They would and they will. What did you do with the leads? I'm walking in that door — you have five seconds to tell me: or you are going to jail.

LEVENE. I . . .

WILLIAMSON. I don't care. You understand? *Where are the leads?* (*Pause.*) Alright. (WILLIAMSON *goes to open the office door.*)

LEVENE. I sold them to Jerry Graff.

WILLIAMSON. How much did you get for them? (*Pause.*) How much did you get for them?

LEVENE. Five thousand. I kept half.

WILLIAMSON. Who kept the other half?

Pause.

LEVENE. Do I have to tell you? (*Pause.* WILLIAMSON *starts to open the door.*) Moss.

WILLIAMSON. *That* was easy *wasn't* it?

Pause.

LEVENE. It was his idea.

WILLIAMSON. *Was* it?

LEVENE. I . . . I'm sure he got more than the five, actually.

WILLIAMSON. Uh huh?

LEVENE. He told me my share was twenty-five.

Pause.

WILLIAMSON. Mmm.

LEVENE. Okay: I, look: I'm going to make it worth your while. I am. I turned this thing around. I closed the *old* stuff, I can do it again. *I'm* the one's going to close 'em. I am! *I* am! Cause I turned this thing a . . . I can do *that,* I can do *anyth* . . . last night. I'm going to tell you, I was ready to Do the Dutch. Moss gets me, 'Do this, we'll get well . . .' Why not? Big fuckin' deal. I'm hoping to get caught. To put me out of my . . . (*Pause.*) But it *taught* me something. What it taught me, that you've got to get *out* there. Big deal. So I wasn't cut out to be a thief. I *was* born for a salesman. And now I'm back, and I got my *balls* back . . . and, you know, John, you have the *advantage* on me now. Whatever it takes to make it right, we'll make it right. We're going to make it right.

WILLIAMSON. I want to tell you something, Shelly. You have a big mouth.

Pause.

LEVENE. What?

WILLIAMSON. You've got a big mouth, and now I'm going to show you an even bigger one. (*He starts toward the* DETECTIVE's *door.*)

LEVENE. Where are you going, John? . . . you can't do that, you
   don't want to do that . . . hold, hold on . . . hold on . . . wait
   . . . wait . . . wait . . . (*He pulls money out of his pockets.*)
   Wait . . . uh, look . . . (*He starts splitting the money.*) Look,
   twelve, twenty, two, twen . . . twenty-five hundred, it's . . .
   take it. (*Pause.*) Take it . . . (*Pause.*) Take it!

WILLIAMSON. No, I don't think so, Shel.

LEVENE. I . . .

WILLIAMSON. No, I think I don't want your money. I think
   you fucked up my office. And I think you're going away.

LEVENE. I . . . what? Are you, are you, that's why . . .? are you
   nuts? I'm . . . I'm going to *close* for you, I'm going to . . .
   (*Thrusting money at him.*) Here, here, I'm going to *make* this
   office . . . I'm going to be back there Number One . . . Hey,
   hey, hey! This is only the beginning . . . List . . . list . . . listen.
   Listen. Just one moment. List . . . here's what . . . here's
   what we're going to do. Twenty per cent. I'm going to give
   you twenty per cent of my sales . . . (*Pause.*) Twenty per
   cent. (*Pause.*) For as long as I am with the firm. (*Pause.*)
   Fifty per cent. (*Pause.*) You're going to be my partner.
   (*Pause.*) Fifty per cent. Of all my sales.

WILLIAMSON. What sales?

LEVENE. What sales . . .? I just *closed* eighty-two *grand* . . . Are
   you fuckin' . . . I'm *back* . . . I'm *back*, this is only the
   beginning.

WILLIAMSON. Only the beginning . . .

LEVENE. Abso . . .

WILLIAMSON. Where have you been, Shelly? Bruce and Harriett
   Nyborg. Do you want to see the *memos* . . .? They're nuts . . .
   they used to call in every week. When I was with Webb. And
   we were selling Arizona . . . they're nuts . . . did you see how
   they were *living*? How can you delude yours . . .

LEVENE. I've got the check . . .

WILLIAMSON. Frame it. It's worthless.

   Pause.

LEVENE. The check's no good?

WILLIAMSON. You stick around I'll pull the memo for you. (*He starts for the door.*) I'm busy now . . .

LEVENE. . . . their check's no good? They're nuts . . .?

WILLIAMSON. Call up the bank. *I* called them.

LEVENE. You did?

WILLIAMSON. I called them when we had the lead . . . four months ago. (*Pause.*) The people are insane. They just like talking to salesmen. (WILLIAMSON *starts for the door.*)

LEVENE. Don't.

WILLIAMSON. I'm sorry.

LEVENE. *Why*?

WILLIAMSON. Because I don't like you.

LEVENE. John: John: . . . my *daughter* . . .

WILLIAMSON. Fuck you.

> ROMA *comes out of the* DETECTIVE's *door.*
> WILLIAMSON *goes in.*

ROMA (*to* WILLIAMSON). *Asshole* . . . (*To* LEVENE:) Guy couldn't find his fuckin' couch the *living-room* . . . Ah, Christ . . . what a day, what a day . . . and I haven't even had a cup of *coffee* . . . Jagoff John opens his mouth he blows my Cadillac . . . (*He sighs.*) I swear . . . it's not a world of men . . . it's not a world of men, Machine . . . it's a world of clock watchers, bureaucrats, office holders . . . What it is, it's a fucked-up world . . . there's no adventure *to* it . . . (*Pause.*) Dying breed. Yes it is. (*Pause.*) We are the members of a dying breed. That's . . . that's . . . I want to talk to you. I've wanted to talk to you for some *time* actually . . . seriously. Did you eat today?

LEVENE. Me?

ROMA. Yes.

LEVENE. No.

ROMA. No? Come on, we're going to swing by the Chinks, we got to talk.

LEVENE. I think I'd better stay here for a while.

ROMA. Okay: Two things, then. One . . . I been thinking about this for a *month,* I said 'the Machine . . . There's a fellow I could *work* with,' never, isn't that funny? I never did a thing. Now: That shit that you were slinging on the guy today was *very* good, and excuse me it isn't even my *place* to *say* that to you that way; I've been on a hot streak, so big deal. What I'm saying, it was *admirable* and, so was the *deal* that you closed. Now listen: there's things I could *learn* from you — you see, I *knew* we'd work well together — Here's what I was thinking: we Team Up. We team up, we go out together, we split everything right down the middle . . .

BAYLEN *sticks his head out of the room.*

BAYLEN. Mr *Levene* . . .?

ROMA. . . . fifty-fifty. Or we could go down the street. You know, we could go *anywhere* . . .

BAYLEN. Would you step in here, please . . .?

ROMA. So let's put it *together*? Okay? (*Pause.*) Shel? Say 'okay'.

LEVENE (*pause*). Hmm . . .

BAYLEN. Mr Levene, I think we have to talk.

ROMA. I'm going to the Chinks. You're done, come down, we're going to smoke a cigarette.

LEVENE. I . . .

BAYLEN *comes over to him and forcefully leads him into the room.*

BAYLEN. . . . get in the room.

ROMA. Hey, hey, hey, *easy,* friend. That's the 'Machine'. That is Shelly The Machine *Lev* . . .

BAYLEN. Come on. Get in the goddamn *room* . . .

LEVENE. I . . .

ROMA. I'll be at the resta . . .

BAYLEN *and* LEVENE *have disappeared into the next room and the door is slammed. Pause.*

Williamson: listen to me: when the *leads* come in . . .
listen to me: when the *leads* come in I want my top two off
the list. For *me*. My usual two. Anything you give *Levene* . . .

WILLIAMSON. . . . I wouldn't worry about it.

ROMA. Well I'm *going* to worry about it, and so are you, so
you shut up and listen. (*Pause.*) I GET HIS ACTION. My
stuff is *mine*, whatever *he* gets, I'm talking half. You put me
in with him.

AARONOW *enters.*

AARONOW. Did they . . .?

ROMA. You understand?

AARONOW. Did they catch . . .?

ROMA. Do you understand? My stuff is mine, his stuff is ours.

WILLIAMSON. Mmm.

AARONOW. Did they find the guy who broke into the office
yet?

ROMA. No. *I* don't know . . .

Pause.

AARONOW. Did the leads come in yet?

ROMA. No.

AARONOW (*settling into a desk chair*). Oh, god I hate this job.

ROMA (*simultaneous with 'job', going out of the office*). I'll be
at the restaurant.